HOW TO DEVELOP
A PROFESSIONAL
PORTFOLIO

2/14

HOW TO DEVELOP A PROFESSIONAL PORTFOLIO

A Manual for Teachers

Dorothy M. Campbell
Pamela Bondi Cignetti
Beverly J. Melenyzer
Diane Hood Nettles
Richard M. Wyman, Jr.

California University of Pennsylvania

Allyn and Bacon
Boston • London • Toronto • Sydney • Tokyo • Singapore

Series Editor: Virginia Lanigan
Editorial Assistant: Nihad Farooq
Editorial-Production Service: Matrix Productions
Cover Designer: Suzanne Harbison
Composition Buyer: Linda Cox
Manufacturing Buyer: Suzanne Lareau

Copyright © 1997 by Allyn & Bacon
A Viacom Company
160 Gould Street
Needham Heights, MA 02194

Library of Congress Cataloging-in-Publication Data

How to develop a professional portfolio : a manual for teachers /
    authors, Dorothy M. Campbell ... [et al.].
        p.   cm.
    ISBN 0-205-26153-1
    1. Teachers--Rating of.   2. Portfolios in education.   3. Teachers--
Employment.   I. Campbell, Dorothy M.
    LB2838.H56   1996
    371.1'44--dc20
                                                            96-16500
                                                    CIP

Printed in the United States of America
10 9 8 7   01 00 99

CONTENTS

Preface   vii

Acknowledgments   ix

1   What You Need to Know about Portfolios   1
Why Portfolios?   1
What Is a Portfolio?   3
How Do I Organize My Portfolio?   4
What Evidence Should I Include in My Portfolio?   5
Who Is the Audience for My Portfolio?   5
How Might I Use My Portfolio?   7

2   Guidelines for Assembling Your Portfolio   9
How to Use This Chapter   9
Creating the Working Portfolio   10
Creating the Presentation Portfolio   13

3   Organization of Portfolios around Teaching Standards   19
How to Use This Chapter   19
How This Chapter Is Organized   20
Knowledge of the Subject Matter   23
Knowledge of Human Development and Learning   27
Adapting Instruction for Individual Needs   31
Multiple Instructional Strategies   35

Classroom Motivation and Management Skills   *39*
Communication Skills   *43*
Instructional Planning Skills   *47*
Assessment of Student Learning   *51*
Professional Commitment and Responsibility   *55*
Partnerships   *59*

4   Artifacts Possibilities   63
    How to Use This Chapter   *63*
    Types of Artifacts   *63*

Appendices   79
    Appendix A: Professional Organizations   *79*
    Appendix B: Artifacts Checklist   *81*

PREFACE

The growing interest among colleges of education in performance assessment and the stiff competition for teaching jobs have resulted in a chorus of voices telling prospective teachers as well as practicing teachers, "You ought to develop a professional portfolio." We in the Elementary/Early Childhood Department at California University of Pennsylvania found ourselves joining this chorus as we became increasingly convinced that our students needed more authentic, broad-based and holistic ways to demonstrate their growing professional competence. A transcript of grades and a score on a national exam seemed inadequate indicators of competence. Moreover, we wanted to give our students a larger measure of control in charting their own professional growth.

We knew little would change unless we moved beyond "ought to"; our students would need specific guidelines for developing a portfolio, and our department would need a structured portfolio assessment process. Since 1993, our department has been engaged in creating these guidelines and structure. The authors of this manual comprise a department committee that has spearheaded these efforts. A version of this manual has been available to majors in our department since that time and has been effective in guiding prospective teachers in developing professional portfolios.

This book presents step-by-step practical procedures and tips on how to organize a professional portfolio to document the achievement of professional goals. It is written primarily for preservice teachers; however, inservice teachers, school districts, or university departments of education can adapt and interpret the guidelines presented to their unique situations.

ACKNOWLEDGMENTS

Appreciation is extended by this committee of authors to all the other members of the Elementary/Early Childhood Department at California University of Pennsylvania and to our dean and associate dean for their assistance, support, and enthusiastic interest in this manual and in the larger challenge of creating for our department a portfolio development and assessment process for our majors.

Elementary/Early Childhood Department Members,
California University of Pennsylvania:
Eileen Aiken
Ronald Christ
Elwin Dickerson
Allan Jacobs
Gary Kennedy
Greg Martin
Phyllis McIlwain
Roger Orr
Anthony Saludis
Caryl Sheffield
John Shimkanin
Jamie Southworth
John Vargo
College of Education and Human Services:
Stephen A. Pavlak, Dean
John R. Young, Associate Dean

We would also like to say thanks to Shannon Snee, Betty Ann Bisher, Kelly Jenkins, and Denise Weaver for their technical assistance. A special note of gratitude goes to Karen Posa for her continued support throughout this long process; finally, our respect and appreciation to our department chairman, Roger Orr, for his vision, enthusiasm, and occasional pizza.

HOW TO DEVELOP
A PROFESSIONAL
PORTFOLIO

1

WHAT YOU NEED
TO KNOW
ABOUT PORTFOLIOS

WHY PORTFOLIOS?

The Superintendent looked over her desk at Kimberly and asked one final question.

"In the last few years, the district has placed a heavy emphasis on cooperative learning in our elementary classrooms. How knowledgeable are you about this instructional strategy, and, if you were hired to fill this position, would you feel comfortable using it in your classroom?"

"Well," said Kimberly, "I feel that I have both a theoretical and practical understanding of cooperative learning. As you can see in my portfolio, I wrote a research paper dealing with the work of Robert Slavin. In it, I describe his three major techniques and their effect on student achievement. I have also included lesson plans using this strategy that I developed and taught during student teaching. The comments by my supervisor and classroom teacher indicate they were successful. I feel that cooperative learning is a very effective instructional technique."

The Superintendent leaned back in her chair.

"Kimberly, you were the only candidate for this position with a well-organized portfolio. Your verbal responses to my questions were excellent but so were those of other candidates. However, you were the only one able to support those responses with concrete examples of your knowledge and experience. Your portfolio shows your competence in all the areas of teaching that we feel are important. I am very impressed. I think you'll be a fine addition to our district."

The preceding scenario makes evident how imperative it is that, as a prospective teacher, you are able to demonstrate to others in concrete ways your teaching competence. Teaching jobs are highly competitive, and therefore creative ways of presenting yourself are essential.

However, prospective employers are not the only ones who will be holding you accountable for proving your competence. State departments of education are increasing requirements for compelling evidence of performance before issuing teacher certification. In addition, in 1987, a National Board for Professional Teaching Standards was formed for the purpose of setting standards for the teaching profession, thus impacting teacher certification. A voluntary national teaching credential is now a real possibility. Many teacher education programs are utilizing measurements of performance as an alternative for evaluating preservice teachers' progress in their professional training. Furthermore, once you obtain a teaching job, you will be periodically evaluated and held accountable for utilizing exemplary teaching practices throughout your professional career.

Traditionally, decontextualized assessments such as test scores and transcript grades have been used to evaluate teachers. However, you will find that these types of assessments do not necessarily reflect the range of abilities that true professionals possess. Teachers are justifiably concerned that assessments and accountability requirements be authentic, broad-based, and impartial. As a professional you will want all of your knowledge and experience to be taken into account when you are evaluated.

One characteristic of excellent teachers is that they learn from every experience and every person they meet. They seek ongoing professional training to refine their practice. They remain current about educational research. They read professional journals and books, attend workshops, and interact with colleagues in order to benefit from the experience of others. They ask endless questions of other people and really listen to the answers. They try out new ideas, reflect on the results, and then discard or adapt the ideas. Often they keep reflective journals. When they travel, they look for opportunities to learn all they can about other places They volunteer in the community, getting to know its people, values, and agencies. When they join groups they tend to be the ones who go to the meetings and do the committee work.

Although teachers know that all these forms of experience have contributed to their becoming effective professionals, most would find it difficult to demonstrate to others exactly how these various experiences have fit into their pattern of professional growth. As you embark on your professional journey, you will probably find that you, too, have many valuable skills and experiences that are difficult to convey in a single test score or course grade. Because these skills and experiences are part of your growing competencies, it is important that you be able to convey them to others as well as to yourself.

A professional portfolio can help. It can be a tool that enables you to make sense out of a myriad of experiences. It also can bring into focus a clear picture of yourself as a growing, changing professional. Equally as significant, it can be a convincing, effective vehicle for you to demonstrate to others in a meaningful way the skills and knowledge you have gained in something as complex as teaching.

WHAT IS A PORTFOLIO?

A portfolio is not merely a file of course projects and assignments, nor is it a scrapbook of teaching memorabilia. A portfolio is an organized, goal-driven documentation of your professional growth and achieved competence in the complex act called teaching. Although it is a collection of documents, a portfolio is tangible evidence of the wide range of knowledge, dispositions, and skills that you possess as a growing professional. What's more, documents in the portfolio are self-selected, reflecting your individuality and autonomy.

There are actually two kinds of portfolios that you will be developing: a working portfolio and a presentation portfolio. A working portfolio is characterized by your ongoing systematic collection of selected work in courses and evidence of community activities. This collection would form a framework for self-assessment and goal setting. Later, you would develop a presentation portfolio by winnowing your collection to samples of your work that best reflect your achieved competence, individuality, and creativity as a professional educator.

What Is a Working Portfolio?

A working portfolio is always much larger and more complete than a presentation portfolio. It contains unabridged versions of the documents you have carefully selected to portray your professional growth. For example, it might contain entire reflective journals, complete units, unique teacher-made materials, and a collection of videos of your teaching. Working portfolios are often stored in a combination of computer disks, notebooks, and even boxes.

What Is a Presentation Portfolio?

A presentation portfolio is compiled for the expressed purpose of giving others an effective and easy-to-read portrait of your professional competence. A presentation portfolio is selective and streamlined because other people usually do not have the time to review all the material in your working portfolio. In making a presentation portfolio, you will find that less is more. For example, since you would be unlikely to take to an interview all your teacher-made learning materials, you might rely on photographs. Most reviewers would not want to assess several videos of your teaching but would be interested in one well-edited and annotated video. Sample pages from a large project would replace an entire project. The two types of portfolios differ in that all documents in a presentation portfolio should be preceded by an explanation of the importance or relevance of the document so that the reviewer understands the context of your work. Because it is important that a presentation portfolio not be cumbersome or unwieldy, we recommend the use of a notebook.

HOW DO I ORGANIZE MY PORTFOLIO?

There is one essential way in which working portfolios and presentation portfolios are alike. From their inception, both need to have a well-established organizational system. There is no one standard way to organize a portfolio, but to be effective it must have a system of organization that is understandable and meaningful to you and other educators. We suggest organizing your portfolio around a set of goals you are trying to achieve. This makes sense when one of your purposes for a portfolio is to demonstrate to others that you are achieving success in meeting standards set for excellence in the teaching profession.

Many professional organizations are setting goals for the teachers of the twenty-first century. These organizations include state departments of education, professional societies such as the National Association for the Education of Young Children or the National Council of Teachers of Mathematics, interagency groups, and university schools of education. Appendix A provides a list of addresses for many professional organizations concerned with standards for teaching. The professional goals established by these organizations are called by a variety of names, including standards, principles, performance domains, outcomes, and competencies. They are all attempts to reflect the knowledge, skills, and dispositions that define excellent teachers and therefore are goals for you as a preservice teacher to achieve.

You should become familiar with a number of documents that outline sets of standards for your discipline, your state, and your own university department. As you study these standards, choose or adapt a set of goals that makes sense to you in your particular situation. Regardless of the goals or standards chosen, everything collected for your portfolio should be organized around the chosen goal statements.

The sample goals or standards used in this book are principles established by the Interstate New Teacher Assessment and Support Consortium

(INTASC).[1] These standards were chosen because of their general applicability for teachers of all disciplines and all levels, preschool to grade 12. It is apparent that engaging in the development of a portfolio organized around a set of goals or standards will greatly facilitate your growth and achievement in the goals identified. Figure 1–1 shows the INTASC standards.

WHAT EVIDENCE SHOULD I INCLUDE IN MY PORTFOLIO?

For every standard, you will include artifacts that demonstrate you have met this principle. An artifact is tangible evidence of knowledge that is gained, skills that are mastered, values that are clarified, or dispositions and attitudes that are characteristic of you. Artifacts cannot conclusively prove the attainment of knowledge, skills, or dispositions, but they provide indicators of achieved competence. For example, lesson and unit plans are pieces of evidence that might provide strong indication of your ability to plan curriculum or use a variety of teaching strategies. A video of your teaching might be a convincing indicator of your ability to manage and motivate a group of students. The same artifact may document more than one standard. Chapter 4 will describe more than fifty possibilities for portfolio artifacts. At first, many artifacts will be collected. Later, artifacts will be selectively placed within each of the standards. Only those artifacts that represent your very best professional work should be included as evidence. Ask yourself: Would I be proud to have my future employer and peer group see this? Is this an example of what my future professional work might look like? Does this represent what I stand for as a professional educator? If not, what can I do to revise or rearrange so that it represents my best efforts?

WHO IS THE AUDIENCE FOR MY PORTFOLIO?

Information contained in the portfolio will be of interest to individuals who will be assessing your performance and measuring your accountability. While a student, your portfolio will be reviewed by your university faculty and advisors. Moreover, your portfolio will be an excellent way for you to intro-

---

[1]Darling–Hammond, L. (Ed.) (1992, September). *Model standards for beginning teacher licensing and development: A resource for state dialogue.* Unpublished draft, Interstate New Teacher Assessment and Support Consortium, Council of Chief State School Officers, Washington, DC.

The standards below were developed by Interstate New Teacher Assessment and Support Consortium (INTASC). The designated headings are ours.

Standard #1 – Knowledge of Subject Matter
The teacher understands the central concepts, tools of inquiry, and structure of the discipline(s) he or she teaches and can create learning experiences that make these aspects of subject matter meaningful for students.

Standard #2 – Knowledge of Human Development and Learning
The teacher understands how children learn and develop, and can provide learning opportunities that support their intellectual, social, and personal development.

Standard #3 – Adapting Instruction for Individual Needs
The teacher understands how students differ in their approaches to learning and creates instructional opportunities that are adapted to diverse learners.

Standard #4 – Multiple Instructional Strategies
The teacher understands and uses a variety of instructional strategies to encourage students' development of critical thinking, problem solving, and performance skills.

Standard #5 – Classroom Motivation and Management Skills
The teacher uses an understanding of individual and group motivation and behavior to create a learning environment that encourages positive social interaction, active engagement in learning, and self-motivation.

Standard #6 – Communication Skills
The teacher uses knowledge of effective verbal, nonverbal, and media communication techniques to foster active inquiry, collaboration, and supportive interaction in the classroom.

Standard #7 – Instructional Planning Skills
The teacher plans instruction based on knowledge of subject matter, students, the community, and curriculum goals.

Standard #8 – Assessment of Student Learning
The teacher understands and uses formal and informal assessment strategies to ensure the continuous intellectual, social, and physical development of the learner.

Standard #9 – Professional Commitment and Responsibility
The teacher is a reflective practitioner who continually evaluates the effects of his or her choices and actions on others (students, parents, and other professionals in the learning community), and who actively seeks out opportunities to grow professionally.

Standard #10 – Partnerships
The teacher fosters relationships with school colleagues, parents, and agencies in the larger community to support students' learning and well-being.

FIGURE 1-1   Model Standards for Beginning Teachers' Licensing and Development

duce yourself to cooperating teachers during field experiences and student teaching. During job interviews, your portfolio is likely to be reviewed by superintendents, principals, teachers, and in some cases even school board members. As you begin your teaching career, your portfolio will be a helpful vehicle for mentors, in-service education coordinators, and other colleagues. In some school districts, a portfolio will be relied on by supervisory staff charting ongoing career development or making promotion decisions. There is also a good possibility that your portfolio will one day be used to facilitate licensing by professional organizations, state agencies, or national consortiums. Most importantly, the portfolio provides you, the author, with an informative and accurate picture of your professional development and growth.

HOW MIGHT I USE MY PORTFOLIO?

In this chapter you have been introduced to a very motivating reason for you to commit time, energy, and thought to developing a portfolio: You will have a high-impact, authentic product by which your professional competence can be judged by others. Before you get into later chapters, which will provide you with detailed steps and examples for developing a portfolio, you might reflect on other ways beyond interviews and certification requirements to use your portfolio to your best advantage.

You will find as you engage in portfolio development that you will gain a much clearer picture of yourself as an emerging professional. Your portfolio will provide a record of quantitative and qualitative growth over time in your selected goal areas or standards. You will have in hand a trail of evidence of your progress in each of your teaching standards. This will give you a gratifying sense of accomplishment and pride and will help you have ever-increasing confidence in your professional abilities.

As you review this record of your professional growth, you will also gain a vision of the big picture. You will more fully understand who you want to be as a professional (as defined by the standards that you choose). Then, as you organize selected artifacts around these standards, you will begin to discern a pattern of how your various course assignments and out-of-class experiences fit into this big picture and contributed to your development.

As you gain more self-understanding, your portfolio will empower you to assume more control over your own future learning. You will be well equipped to collaborate with professors in individualizing assignments or with advisors in planning courses of study. You will have a greatly expanded resume to be used to introduce yourself to cooperating teachers in student teaching and field experiences classes. You and your cooperating teachers now have a tool for determining the most appropriate teaching experiences for you. As you can see, when you reflect on the portrait your portfolio provides, you will be well positioned to set realistic and meaningful goals for yourself. Choices that exist in your coursework, field work, and self-initiated learning opportunities will now have a meaningful focus.

In addition, the portfolio may be used by a university program as a way to keep students and faculty focused on goals or standards valued by the program. Students will be continually reflecting on the standards as their portfolios provide an authentic and meaningful way to be assessed professionally. Portfolios will provide faculty members with evidence of their effectiveness in preparing students to meet selected standards. Portfolios can help with program evaluation and bring to light the need for new courses, revised course syllabi, or policy changes.

It should now be clear why having a professional portfolio is of value, what a portfolio is, what goes into one, and who would be interested in seeing it. Now you are ready to look at portfolio development in a more specific way. Chapter 2 will explain step-by-step procedures for creating both a working portfolio and a presentation portfolio. In Chapter 3, the INTASC standards are explained with scenarios that illustrate various professional growth opportunities and how to document them in a portfolio. In Chapter 4, more than fifty possible artifacts are described, which will help you see possibilities for a variety of ways to portray your skills and knowledge.

2

GUIDELINES FOR ASSEMBLING YOUR PORTFOLIO

HOW TO USE THIS CHAPTER

Creating a portfolio is not difficult—it just takes time and personal reflection. As stated in Chapter 1, the process of developing a portfolio begins early in your professional career, when you start to collect documents and pieces of your work that exemplify your capabilities as a teacher. This collection, called the working portfolio, will be extensive; it will contain everything you have done that you judge to be worthy of saving. Eventually you will need to produce a presentation portfolio. This is for the purpose of showcasing only portions of your work for a prospective employer or certification officer. The presentation portfolio is streamlined; only the most pertinent material for the position is organized and displayed. Both types of portfolios are organized in the same manner: Documents are categorized by standards that you have adopted. These standards are goals that will guide you throughout your teacher preparation work, or your career, or both. This chapter will give you some practical information on putting together both types of portfolios.

The first section of the chapter contains information to help you organize your collection of documents for a working portfolio. This will be an ongoing project as you complete your teacher education program or prepare for certification. The second section is designed to help you produce a presentation portfolio that is uniquely yours, at the same time documenting important information that will be examined by prospective employers or certification officers. Included are questions you may have about assembling your portfolio. The answers provide guidelines that are important; however, feel free to use your own creativity in developing a portfolio that portrays you as an individual as well as a professional educator.

CREATING THE WORKING PORTFOLIO

Where Do I Start?

Choose a way to store your documents. The working portfolio will contain a multitude of artifacts, many of which will be cumbersome. Decide how you want to house your artifacts. This portfolio needs to be easily accessible, expandable, and organized. You may want to use a large file box. Office supply stores carry cardboard "banker's boxes," which are easily assembled and easy to carry around. You can put all your artifacts in one box, with files dividing it into sections. If you prefer, you can use several smaller boxes, one for each standard you are documenting. Other options are to use a large notebook that can be divided into sections or a file drawer in a cabinet that has plenty of space for several folders.

Consider the types of artifacts you will be saving when making this decision. Will you be using a number of videotapes or computer disks? Will you be making teaching materials you will want to save? Will you be taking photographs of projects? Do you tend to write lengthy papers? These types of artifacts require space as well as special types of handling when organizing and storing them for long periods of time.

How Do I Document the Standards?

Create a Filing System

Divide the Portfolio into Sections.   Your portfolio will contain several sections, each of which will correspond to a standard you have adopted. In the examples provided in this book, each section will reflect one of the ten standards outlined by the Interstate New Teacher Assessment and Support Consortium (INTASC). These standards are descriptions of teacher behaviors agreed upon by a group of educators in the consortium; they were developed to be compatible with other national standards for certification. Your school program has probably adopted a set of goals or standards that guides its students or teachers. Such a set of goals is useful for guiding preservice teachers through their teacher preparation program at the university or for guiding inservice teachers as they apply for recertification. Adopt a set of standards appropriate for your situation and organize the portfolios around these standards.

Your portfolio needs to document that you have indeed met your chosen goals. Therefore, organize your portfolio in such a way that these standards are easily identified. If you are using a file box or expanding file for your working portfolio, create a file or section for each standard. You may want to color code the files to facilitate easier management. If you are using a notebook to house your working portfolio, the best way to do this is to include tab pages for each standard, dividing your portfolio into as many sections as there are standards.

Label Each Section.   Make sure that each section of your portfolio clearly identifies a standard statement. Create a shortened version of each standard. For example, in this manual, Standard #8 is called "Assessment of Student Learning." You could call this "Assessment" or "Assessment Skills." If you are using a file box or file cabinet, type the shortened version of the standard statement on a file label to attach to the file tab. If you are using a notebook with tab sheets, type it directly on the tab. You can purchase a variety of types of tab pages at an office supply store. Some will require you to type headings on small white tabs and insert them into plastic sleeves. If you use these, make sure the tabs stay in the plastic sleeves. Others allow you to type directly onto the tab sheet or a table of contents sheet.

In addition, a copy of the entire standard statement should be placed somewhere at the beginning of the section. You can do this by typing the standard on a large label sticker and affixing it to the front of the file folder or tab page. Or, simply type it on the first page of the section. This is important because reading the standard statements again and again will help familiarize you with them and thus help you choose appropriate documents for each.

Examine the Possibilities for Documentation
Study the suggestions and examples in this manual. Sample standard statements are listed and explained in Chapter 3 along with real-life examples. In Chapter 4, many possible artifacts are listed. These are artifacts that could be used to document any set of standards. They have been defined and explained, so that you can get some idea of what is meant by terms such as "video scenario critiques" or "theme studies," and also so that you can see the possibilities for documenting standards. Check your files for any of these artifacts and save them. Many of them probably reflect class assignments given in your methods classes. However, you may want to create artifacts. For example, perhaps you have not already written a philosophy statement, even though you have a very clear idea of your philosophy of education. Therefore, composing one for the purpose of including it in the portfolio would be a wise idea. You may also need to add to artifacts you already have. Suppose

you attended a professional meeting or lecture but did not write a reaction paper or take notes. Now is a good time to write a brief critique of what you saw and heard and add it to your file for the portfolio.

Become a Pack Rat

If you have not already done so, begin collecting. Make your file box, cabinet, or notebook with its tabs and start putting examples of class assignments and other artifacts in these categories right away. (This is necessary because you will want to see if there are any standards for which you do not have artifacts, something that is discussed in the next section.) Remember that you can use an artifact in more than one section because several types of artifacts may document more than one standard. If this happens, photocopy the artifact and highlight the part that specifically addresses the standard. One note of caution: Use this photocopying and highlighting idea sparingly. Duplicating too many artifacts will make your portfolio look as if you do not use a variety of experiences.

As you file each of your artifacts under a standard, make brief notes about why you have filed the document under that particular standard. These notes can be used later when you are ready to create your presentation portfolio. At that time, you will need to write a "rationale statement" for each artifact. This is a brief statement that explains why the artifact you chose for the standard is appropriate and how the artifact showcases your competence in that area. From the standard statement, use specific descriptors that will jar your memory and connect the artifact to the standard. You may want to write these notes on an index card and clip the card to the document. Figure 2–1 shows an example of notes written for a case study that could be used to document INTASC Standard #2.

Look for Holes

Standards that are not well documented by your artifacts will become evident as you collect and categorize materials. Keep the standards in mind as you

---

Standard #2 – Case Study
- Shows how a child's language developed from infancy
- Written over a 3-month period
- Identifies some stages of language development
- Shows how the child learned several new words

FIGURE 2–1   Example of a Note Card to Attach to the Artifact When Filing

take other courses or participate in professional activities. Whenever you have assignment choices, such as journal article critiques to write or projects to complete in your university coursework, think about the standards you need to work on. Consider how you can make this assignment document your "missing standard." Look for meetings to attend, journals to read or subscribe to, organizations to join, extra credit assignments to complete, community activities to volunteer for, personal diaries to write, or any number of activities that can be recorded and included in your portfolio. You may also want to ask your professors for guidance in this area. See if they have suggestions for ways to make your class assignments document a particular standard while at the same time completing the requirements for their courses.

One of the ways you can manage the documentation of standards is with the Artifact Checklist in Appendix B. This is a list of all the artifacts defined in Chapter 4. As you use them in your portfolio, mark them with a date on the checklist. Be sure to use a pencil, because as time passes, you may choose to remove some artifacts from your portfolio; thus, you will need to erase the date mark. This checklist allows you (and your professor or advisor) to see at a glance the standards you need to work on. It also allows you to quickly assess your use of artifacts. Are you depending on some types of artifacts more than others? You may want to diversify your artifacts to more clearly document your repertoire of abilities.

CREATING THE PRESENTATION PORTFOLIO

Why Create Another Portfolio?

Your working portfolio is just that—one that works for you. When you have reached a stage in your professional career that calls for showcasing your abilities to someone else, you will need a presentation portfolio. You will gather this collection of documents specifically for a job you are seeking or a type of teaching certificate you need. The documents can be pulled from the collection in your working portfolio and placed appropriately into a presentation portfolio.

How Do I Prepare the Presentation Portfolio?

Use a Container That Works for You
For your presentation portfolio, you can experiment with many types of containers such as notebooks, expanding files, folders, or portfolio satchels. Consider the types of artifacts you have collected. If you have electronic documents such as videotapes or computer disks, you will need to display

them so they are easily accessible and neatly organized. When the portfolio is complete, you want your reader to be able to open it and read it without struggling with pages, binders, or pockets. Therefore, use a container that is large enough to house all your documents. Most people choose a large notebook. Generally, 2" or 3" three-ring binders are fine. Color is not important; neatness is. Browse through an office supply store for your notebook. Many stores carry a style with a plastic insert cover that you can personalize with your name and a title. Pockets for storage of electronic documents are also available and can be inserted easily in most types of notebooks. One note of caution: Do not use a notebook that is too big, or your portfolio will look empty.

Identify the Standards

Remember that your prospective employer or certification officer does not know what each of the standard titles means. As with the working portfolio, you will need to label each section with an abbreviated title for the standard and include a copy of the standard statement.

Be Selective in Choosing Artifacts

As in the working portfolio, you will gather artifacts that document your abilities in each of the standards you have adopted. However, most employers do not have a great deal of time to peruse portfolios and are interested in only the most pertinent information about your abilities. This means you must be selective in what you choose for the presentation portfolio. Two or three artifacts in each section is all you need. Choose artifacts that exemplify the type of position or certificate you are seeking. For example, if you are interviewing for a first grade teaching position, select as many examples of your work in the area of early childhood education as possible.

Rationalize Your Artifact Choices

In each section of your portfolio, you will insert various artifacts that document your proficiency and experience for that standard. Readers of your portfolio will not necessarily know why you included these artifacts. Therefore, you need to include a rationale for each artifact in the notebook. Type a brief statement explaining your justification for including this artifact in the portfolio for this particular standard. This statement should be no longer than one page. Make sure you explain why this is an example of your best work, specifically for this standard. Your rationale should show the reader that you know what you are capable of doing in terms of meeting the standard. Be specific about showcasing your abilities. (This is difficult for some people. They feel as if they are bragging.) Do not simply summarize the document. When writing a rationale statement, answer these questions:

1. What is the artifact?
2. Why is it filed under this standard?
3. What does it say about my growing competence?

To organize your portfolio and make artifacts and rationale statements clearly identifiable, add a cover sheet for each artifact you include. This sheet lists the name of the artifact and the date it was written. If applicable, list the course number for the class in which you completed the assignment. Then, type the rationale statement for the artifact. Figure 2–2 shows an example of the cover sheet with a rationale statement included.

Present Your Artifacts Professionally
Remember that this portfolio will represent you as a professional, often in your absence. It may be the first impression an administrator has of you. You will want to make sure your first impression is a good one. Therefore, carefully consider all that goes in this notebook or file. Listed below are questions to ask yourself as you check your work.

1. Are spelling and grammar in Standard English?
2. Is all work typed? All cover sheets, tabs, and documents that you create for the portfolio, and the cover letter, should be typed, preferably on a word processor. Make sure your printer ribbon or laser printer produces

---

Artifact for Standard #5: Classroom Motivation and Management

Name of Artifact: Journal Article Critique
Date: May 2, XXXX
Course: EDE 201 – Foundations of Education
Rationale Statement:
   I have included this journal article critique on ethnocentrism under Standard #5. I feel the article belongs under this standard because ethnocentrism can be very self-motivating and would be part of my classroom. The sharing of different cultures, other than on holidays and special occasions, can help break barriers between cultures. This article demonstrates my position on the subject, how I would implement it in my classroom, and how it can be a positive part of my classroom management.

FIGURE 2–2   Example of a Cover Sheet for an Artifact
Taken from a Class Assignment

clear, dark print. Remember that prospective employers will notice your ability to type as well as your proficiency with computer word processing. The only exceptions to typed work would be artifacts such as journals, students' papers, or observation logs that were not originally typed.

3. Is everything about your overall presentation consistent? Are lines on your cover sheets either single spaced or double spaced consistently throughout?

4. Is your work neat? Avoid use of whiteout or erasures.

5. Is your organization easy to follow? Do you have a table of contents that clearly identifies all parts of the portfolio?

How Do I Make the Presentation Portfolio Unique?

Your presentation portfolio will be unique because it reflects your abilities, your strengths, your professionalism. No one else will have a portfolio like yours because you have written all the documents in the notebook. Your prospective employers will be able to see very quickly what you know about teaching and what you believe about education. Listed below are ways to make the portfolio more personalized. Perhaps you can think of ways to organize it that are not stated in this manual.

Be Creative
You may wish to add touches of creativity such as pertinent artwork, photographs, or famous quotations. Your cover pages for each of the artifacts would be good places for these. You can also be creative with the cover of your portfolio, making sure to include all necessary identifying information. Another way to add creativity is to develop the portfolio around a theme. (One we have seen is a portfolio that depicted its writer as a traveler on a journey down the road of professional life.) Whatever you do, keep this simple. You do not want to detract from the work you are trying to showcase, nor do you want to appear as if you are trying to hide incompetence.

Identify Yourself
At the beginning of your portfolio in a well-marked section, include a cover letter. Listed below are guidelines.

1. Introduce yourself.

2. Describe the position you are seeking and tell why you believe you are a good candidate for the position.

3. Describe some of your experiences pertinent to the position.

4. Point out specific areas of the portfolio that are particularly exemplary. (Do your homework on this. Find out what types of experiences are valued in the school or district to which you are applying. Include examples of these in your portfolio and make sure the reader knows that they are there.)
5. If you wish, include a photograph and a biographical sketch.

You may also want to take your portfolio to your campus career placement office and ask for suggestions on the best ways to reflect the position you are seeking.

Include Traditional Documents

Most administrators are interested in looking at specific documents that synthesize your abilities and have, over the years, been useful in helping them screen applicants. Clearly label and include these at the beginning of your portfolio:

1. Resume
2. Three letters of recommendation
3. Student teaching evaluations
4. Certification documents (copy of certificate, teacher exam scores, transcripts)
5. Philosophy of education statement

Remember, the portfolio portrays you as an individual and as a professional. It shows evidence of your own personal insights into your experiences and that you have reflected on what you can do. In short, it is your showcase; use it to your advantage.

3

ORGANIZATION OF PORTFOLIOS AROUND TEACHING STANDARDS

HOW TO USE THIS CHAPTER

The art and science of teaching is a complex and challenging activity that cannot be totally and succinctly described by any set of goals, standards, or analysis of duties. However, for the purpose of charting and demonstrating professional growth through a portfolio, some system of categories is needed, imperfect though it may be. You are encouraged to select or develop your own set of standards or goals from the many available through universities, state departments of education, and national professional organizations. Indeed, your university program or school district may have a list of goals, competencies, or outcome statements that you may be asked to use as your standards for teaching. If not, refer to Appendix A for a list of organizations that have authored sets of teaching standards. Or, you may wish to adopt or adapt the set used as an example in this textbook.

For the purposes of providing a working example of a portfolio, we have chosen a set of standards or principles developed by the Chief State School Officers' Consortium on licensing, INTASC. The standards are chosen because they were developed by studying standards from many professional associations and the National Board for Professional Teaching. These standards are a general or core set of expectations for all teaching, written in terms of performance and knowledge. Therefore, they have wide applicability. Furthermore, these standards are receiving wide acceptance and use.

If you choose to organize your portfolio around the INTASC standards, you will find this chapter handy. Each of the ten standards is explained and depicted in a real-life scenario. Then, you are shown a sample portfolio cover sheet that could be used with artifacts to document each standard. Therefore, you will be able to read each standard, understand what it means, and picture it in practice.

If you are not using the INTASC standards but have adopted another set of standards instead, this chapter will also be useful to you. Exemplary teaching behaviors are somewhat universally understood. Therefore, the set of standards you have chosen will have concepts similar to the INTASC standards and, in some cases, the same wording. For example, standards offered by the National Board for Professional Teaching Standards for early childhood teachers contain a standard called "Understanding Young Children." The concept of gaining and applying knowledge of child development is the specific teaching behavior outlined in this standard. It is essentially the same concept as INTASC Standard #2, "Knowledge of Human Development and Learning." Because Standard #2 is described and depicted in this chapter, you will want to read that section carefully to gain insights into that area of teaching. Do this for all the standards in your set of goals. You can refer to Figure 1–1 in Chapter 1 and compare your standard statements to the INTASC standards. Then, return to this chapter and read the examples that apply to your teaching situation. Although the scenarios may not portray actual experiences you have had, they will help you picture opportunities for documenting your professional growth.

HOW THIS CHAPTER IS ORGANIZED

Chapter 3 is organized in this manner:

1. Statement of the Standard
   In turn, each of the ten standards or principles for effective teaching as stated by INTASC is presented.
2. Explanation of the Standard
   A short explanation of the standard is provided to add clarity. If you are not using INTASC standards, this explanation of each standard will help you determine similarities and differences between your chosen goals and the ones described here.
3. Teaching Scenario
   Examples typical of preservice teachers' activities both inside and outside college classrooms are presented. Examples are used from four levels of teaching: early childhood, elementary, middle school, and secondary. The scenarios illustrate situations in which professional activities are

indicators of achievement of the standards. Such illustrations will help you relate your set of standards, whether from INTASC or not, to your everyday experiences as a preservice teacher.

4. Sample Cover Sheets for Artifacts

   Following each scenario is a sample cover sheet for artifacts that could document achieved competence in a particular standard. Included in these sample cover sheets are rationale statements, which explain how the artifact documents that particular standard. Because writing these statements is typically the most difficult part of your portfolio development, you will want to pay close attention to them. You may want to use them as models for your own rationale statements in your portfolio.

Remember, all of the material presented in this chapter is for the purpose of example and not meant to imply any view of a single correct way to teach or document professional growth in a portfolio.

KNOWLEDGE OF SUBJECT MATTER

Standard #1

The teacher understands the central concepts, tools of inquiry, and structures of the discipline(s) he or she teaches and can create learning experiences that make these aspects of subject matter meaningful for students.

Explanation of the Standard

Knowledge of subject matter is universally considered an essential attribute for effective teaching and successful learning. The most meaningful and lasting learning occurs when knowledge is constructed by individual students. The role of the teacher is to help learners build their own knowledge through acting on materials and engaging in meaningful experiences. To create these experiences, teachers must possess an in-depth understanding of major concepts, assumptions, debates, processes of inquiry, and ways of knowing that are central to the disciplines they teach.

Knowledge of subject matter also implies an understanding of inquiry used in various disciplines. Inquiry training lets students experience the same process actual scientists go through when attempting to explain a puzzling phenomenon. Employing methods such as inquiry training in the classroom allows teachers to engage learners in generating knowledge and testing hypotheses according to the methods of inquiry and standards of evidence used in the discipline.

In every classroom, it is critical that the teacher evaluate resources and curriculum materials for their comprehensiveness, accuracy, and usefulness for representing particular ideas and concepts. Subject matter knowledge would be essential for the selection and evaluation of curriculum materials and resources.

To illustrate "Knowledge of Subject Matter," the following scenario describes how a student in a social studies methods class developed a unit of study centered around a diary written by a thirteen-year-old girl.

Teaching Scenario

Charlie is a junior education major enrolled in a course called "Teaching Social Studies in the Middle School." A requirement of the course is the development of a unit of study. Charlie has a particular interest in American history, so he decides to do an eighth-grade unit on the Oregon Trail.

Charlie begins his work by reviewing how the topic is dealt with in a traditional social studies curriculum. He examines several eighth-grade social studies texts and finds that the Oregon Trail experience is covered very briefly. Charlie is also dissatisfied with the manner in which the subject is treated: primarily through names, dates, and facts. Charlie would like his students to gain an understanding and appreciation of what the four-month journey was like for those individuals and families who made the long and dangerous trip.

Charlie learned from his professor that, according to the research, children benefit most from forms of narrative history that involve the particular—that is, where a person or small group copes with a particular problem in a particular place at a particular time and under a particular set of circumstances. This type of historical material is most commonly found in original source materials such as journals, diaries, letters, biographies, and in historical fiction.

As a result of his knowledge, Charlie decides to focus his unit of study around a diary written during the overland crossing by a thirteen-year-old girl. The regular social studies textbook, rather than being the primary source of information, will become one of many secondary resource materials.

The unit is designed so that Charlie's students travel the Oregon Trail along with the young girl. They read her words describing the daily routine, the blazing heat, the lack of water, the river crossings, contact with Native Americans, and so forth. Charlie's students can share the joy of this young girl when she and her family finally reach Oregon.

Charlie lists the major concepts the unit will cover, designs appropriate corresponding instructional activities, and lists necessary materials. He describes in some detail how he plans to begin the unit and a culminating activity to provide closure.

Charlie is pleased with the finished product. Apparently the instructor is also pleased, for Charlie receives favorable comments. Charlie decides that his unit would be an excellent choice to include in his portfolio. A copy of his cover sheet and rationale statement follows.

Sample Cover Sheet

Artifact for Standard #1: Knowledge of Subject Matter

Name of Artifact: Oregon Trail Unit
Date: October 2, **XXXX**
Course: EDE 306 – Teaching of Social Studies in the Middle School
Rationale Statement:

    I have included this unit of study in my portfolio to document my knowledge of the subject matter. The topic of the unit is the Oregon Trail. The subject is primarily dealt with through the use of a diary of a young girl who made the crossing in 1849. The current research on how children best learn history indicates that using a primary source document such as a diary would be a particularly effective technique. Children best relate to historical events through some kind of narrative. Learning about the Oregon Trail experience through the words of someone close to their own age would be interesting and enjoyable for my students. This unit is historically accurate and is constructed in agreement with the current research on how to effectively teach history to children. I believe it documents my knowledge of the subject matter.

KNOWLEDGE OF HUMAN DEVELOPMENT AND LEARNING

Standard #2

The teacher understands how children learn and develop, and can provide learning opportunities that support their intellectual, social, and personal development.

Explanation of the Standard

A teacher working with a particular group of children or adolescents quickly realizes how each individual is unique. Differing personalities, learning abilities, interests, and skills make clear the wide variation in students of approximately the same age. And yet, in spite of wide differences, common characteristics unite students within an age group. Thus, although children and adolescents grow and develop at different rates and with varied abilities, there are predictable patterns and sequences to their development.

Understanding these patterns, sequences, and stages of development is essential groundwork for a teacher making decisions about the content and methods of educating a group of students. Educational practice, to be effective, must be rooted in the rapidly advancing research and theory of human development and learning. Often such theory cannot be translated directly into teaching practice. However, when the teacher has a broad understanding of how people learn and develop, this knowledge can be useful in making logical hypotheses in how best to understand and thus respond to an individual student or group of students.

As teachers test their hypotheses in the classroom, they must carefully observe the responses of students and the effects of their curricular choices. Rather than "covering material," teachers must evaluate the quality of the understanding of the content and the developmental appropriateness for the instructional strategies used. Thus, teachers gain knowledge from two sources about how students learn and develop: the fields of human development and psychology, and their own observations of students and reflections about their teaching. The following scenario depicts how a college student uses a study of Piaget's theory of child development to demonstrate her competence in "Knowledge of Human Development and Learning."

Teaching Scenario

Stacey is a sophomore elementary education major. As part of the General Education requirement, Stacey has taken a course in educational psychology.

The work of many psychologists and learning theorists is dealt with in class (e.g. David Ausubel, Benjamin Bloom, Lawrence Kohlberg, Jean Piaget, Erik Erikson). Students are assigned to write a paper about the work and contributions to education of one person discussed in class. Stacey selects Jean Piaget as a subject for her paper.

Stacey begins the paper by presenting background information on Piaget. She reports on his early studies in biology and how he became interested in child development. She discusses the principal concepts of Piaget's theory: schemes, assimilation, accommodation, and equilibration. The bulk of the paper, however, discusses Piaget's four stages of cognitive development: sensorimotor, preoperational, concrete operational, and formal operational. She states that Piaget believed that all children pass through these stages in order, and no child can skip a stage, although different children pass through the stages at somewhat different rates.

Stacey describes the approximate age of children at each stage of development. She also details the cognitive capabilities of children at any one stage. For instance, at the preoperational stage, Stacey notes that children can now arrange things in order according to one attribute such as size or weight. This means that children can line up sticks from smallest to largest. Stacey also lists learning activities commonly used in elementary classrooms that illustrate this ability. Stacey concludes her paper by summarizing criticisms and revisions of Piaget's theory.

Stacey's professor returns the paper with favorable comments. She is impressed with Stacey's research, her writing skills, and her ability to relate Piaget's theory to classroom instruction. She feels the paper indicates that Stacey has a sound understanding of both Piaget's work and his contributions to educational practice. Because of her interest in the subject and the professor's positive evaluation, Stacey decides to include this paper in her portfolio. Her cover sheet and rationale statement are shown here.

Sample Cover Sheet

Artifact for Standard #2: Knowledge of Human Development and Learning

Name of Artifact: Research Paper on Jean Piaget
Date: October 23, XXXX
Course: PSY 208 – Educational Psychology
Rationale Statement:

To document my knowledge of human development, I have selected a research paper I wrote for a class in educational psychology. The subject of the paper was Jean Piaget. I described his four stages of cognitive development and common tasks children at each stage can accomplish. I also described classroom activities that illustrate a child's cognitive ability. I concluded the paper by discussing criticisms of Piaget's theory. I have also included with this paper the positive comments my professor made concerning my work. The research I conducted for this paper and my ability to relate Piaget's work to classroom practice demonstrate my knowledge of child development.

ADAPTING INSTRUCTION FOR INDIVIDUAL NEEDS

Standard #3

The teacher understands how students differ in their approaches to learning and creates instructional opportunities that are adapted to diverse learners.

Explanation of the Standard

There are broad differences in students and the skills they bring to the learning environment. These differences include varied learning styles, diverse cultural backgrounds, and exceptionality in learning. The effective teacher understands how children differ in their development and approaches to learning and is able to adapt strategies and environments to meet specific needs of children. Therefore, a major role of the teacher is to assess each student's developmental levels and abilities in all areas and match learning environments and experiences appropriately. To fulfill this role, a teacher must be an astute observer of students and a professional who can use observational data to diagnose, guide, and instruct. Further, the teacher must design instruction that helps use students' strengths as the basis for their growth. In this classroom, students are valued for their uniqueness and they learn to respect this in one another. The classroom environment then becomes a learning community in which individual differences are respected.

As students' differences become clear, the teacher might adjust task assignments, time allowed, circumstances for work, and communication and response modes for individual students. In some instances, the teacher will participate in and assist other professionals in family-centered assessment and in the development and implementation of individualized plans for children with special developmental and learning needs. To further explain how instruction can be adapted to individual needs, the following scenario describes how a student teacher worked with students with special needs to help them complete a class assignment.

Teaching Scenario

Jess is a student teacher in Mr. Addlestein's tenth-grade English class. At the beginning of the semester, he has a conference with Mr. Addlestein and discovers that there are three students with disabilities in his class, and a fourth student is learning English as a second language (ESL). Jess begins to think about ways in which he can adapt instruction to meet the needs of all students in this class.

During a unit on biographies and autobiographies, Jess decides to use process writing to have all students write their own autobiographies. He issues written contracts and conducts conferences with each student to make a tentative time line for completing each step of the writing process. The four students are offered extra help. At least two extra conferences are planned, and each student is assigned a peer tutor. All students are encouraged to use childhood photographs, magazine pictures, newspaper articles and headlines, or their own creative artwork to help express their ideas for writing the autobiography. Jess feels that this will especially help the students make clear what they want to say in their autobiographies.

Jess decides to include this information in his portfolio for Standard #3. In the tabbed section, he includes a copy of the written contracts made with one of the four special needs students, along with his anecdotal notes made during writing conferences. He also includes a copy of the autobiography written by this student. In front of all this, he inserts a cover page, which includes a rationale statement similar to the following example.

Sample Cover Sheet

Artifact for Standard #3: Adapting Instruction for Individual Needs

Name of Artifact: Results of Writing Process with Students Having
    Special Needs
Date: September 18, XXXX
Course: EDE 461 – Student Teaching
Rationale Statement:

During my student teaching, I learned that my class included four students with special needs, including one who is ESL. To ensure that these students could successfully complete a writing assignment, I needed to adapt my plans to their needs. Therefore, I wrote contracts with them that allowed for extra time, if needed, and planned at least two extra writing conferences. A sample contract and the conference notes on one student are included in this section. During those conferences, I asked this ESL student to bring pictures from magazines and newspapers that he especially liked and reminded him of home. We discussed these, and I taught him several new words this way. Editing and revising were encouraged through his specially assigned peer tutor as well as during our conferences. My anecdotal notes, which I include here, were taken during our writing conferences and show the progress he made over the course of the assignment. His end product was successful and shows evidence of growth. It is also included in this section.

I feel these documents show my ability to create a learning experience that would meet the special needs of a student. I knew that the plans I made for most of the rest of the class would not allow this student to have success with the assignment. Therefore, I tailored the assignment so that he could be successful and grow intellectually as well as socially.

MULTIPLE INSTRUCTIONAL STRATEGIES

Standard #4

The teacher understands and uses a variety of instructional strategies to encourage students' development of critical thinking, problem solving, and performance skills.

Explanation of the Standard

Teachers deal daily with many complexities, including differences among their students in terms of abilities, attitudes, and learning preferences. For these widely varying students, there are multiple goals and objectives to be met, including those dealing with content, basic skills, problem solving, attitudes, dispositions, and critical thinking skills. It is clear that no routine or "pet" teaching approach can effectively meet all of these needs. Effective teachers draw from a wide repertoire of instructional strategies and models, adjusting their choices to meet their intended objectives and the needs of particular students.

There are many instances in which the most efficient and effective way to teach certain kinds of knowledge is through expository teaching or teacher-directed, step-by-step learning. In such cases, direct instruction, presentations, and skills practice are appropriate. However, there are many other times when methods that appear time consuming yield the greatest results in the long run. When students are given the time and materials to be active investigators, they are able to construct a basic framework of knowledge within which to expand their understanding.

Learning for understanding often requires experimentation, problem solving, collaboration, and manipulation of physical objects. Therefore, teachers need models of teaching that include inquiry learning, cooperative learning, concept attainment, and class discussions. These models have as a goal the formation of cognitive structures including concepts, generalizations, dispositions, and understandings rather than simple attainment of specific facts or mastery of discrete skills. As teachers understand the wide variety of instructional strategies available, they will be better able to choose and combine them to integrate affective and cognitive development and to educate for understanding, both of content and of self. Such understandings are exemplified in the example that follows. This is an actual university classroom scenario in which the preservice teacher was investigating ways to teach important concepts to preschoolers.

Teaching Scenario

Erica is an undergraduate enrolled in a course dealing with the content and methods of teaching mathematics in early childhood classrooms. Erica is a member of a small group of students assigned to do an in-depth investigation of developmentally appropriate ways to teach geometric shapes and spatial concepts to children ages three to six (K–3). Erica's group is to present its findings to the total class.

Very soon into the research, Erica and her fellow students realize that young children would learn geometric shapes and spatial concepts best by actively manipulating a wide variety of materials designed to provide extensive and active practice with these concepts. Erica's group begins gathering commercially made manipulatives. The group members also make several teaching materials and games, including bingo, shape twister, a spatial obstacle course, and flannel board story figures that teach spatial and shape concepts. Lastly, Erica's group finds pieces of children's literature as well as computer programs appropriate for teaching children geometric shapes and spatial concepts.

Erica and her group realize that the use of manipulatives by themselves is not enough; they must be accompanied by instructional strategies that promote active inquiry learning. Their research shows them that the teacher facilitates the learning by providing children with opportunities to explore the materials. The teacher guides them through their play by using inductive questioning, encouraging cooperative problem solving, and modeling appropriate vocabulary for new concepts.

To reinforce their learning of these instructional strategies, Erica and her team members visit a local preschool and observe the teachers. They take notes on the types of questions the teachers ask as children experiment with manipulatives. These questions enable the children to induce concepts on their own; thus, they are actively constructing their own knowledge. Erica and her teammates also pay close attention to the way in which the teachers model problem solving for the youngsters and the way in which they explain new concepts and vocabulary. All of this information is included in an observation log, so that Erica and the rest of the group can outline specific instructional strategies to be used with their manipulatives.

These teaching strategies and the materials that accompany them are presented to the total class. Erica's group decides to present these materials through learning centers, much the way materials would be organized for young children. Each set of materials contains a description of the types of questions to ask while the children are playing and the types of problems to ask children to solve.

Erica is proud of what she has learned and the teaching materials she has designed and collected. She decides to document this work for her portfolio by taking pictures of the learning stations on the day of the class presentation. She also prepares descriptions and sketches of the teacher-made materials she designed along with the descriptions of teaching strategies for active inquiry learning. Lastly, Erica prepares a bibliography of the children's literature, computer software, and resource books her group identified. All of this goes into her portfolio, and Erica is careful to give credit to her fellow group members where appropriate. She writes a rationale statement for these documents that is included on the following cover sheet.

Sample Cover Sheet

Artifact for Standard #4: Multiple Instructional Strategies

Name of Artifact: Teaching Math Concepts to Primary Children
Date: November 12, **XXXX**
Course: ECE 315 – Math Content and Methods in Early Childhood
Rationale Statement:

In fulfilling a class assignment to investigate methods and materials used to teach geometric and spatial concepts, I have demonstrated that I can identify instructional strategies that promote inquiry learning. With three peers, I investigated ways to question students so that they learn inductively as well as ways to model problem solving and concept development. This investigation took place in a preschool classroom in which we observed exemplary teachers using these teaching strategies. I found developmentally appropriate math materials that are commercially available and would actively engage students. I also demonstrated my ability to design teacher-made math materials that are versatile, durable, attractive, and age appropriate. These materials were designed to be used by small groups of students and would invite cooperative, hands-on learning. In addition, I was able to find computer programs and pieces of children's literature to help teach the concepts under consideration.

In presenting these strategies and materials to my class, I prepared clear, understandable descriptions of the types of questions and modeling to use when teaching these concepts through inquiry learning. In addition, I prepared concise directions for using the learning materials. To document my abilities, I have included pictures of the materials, narratives that describe them and their accompanying teaching strategies, the observation log that documents investigation, and a bibliography of materials that the other group members and I identified to teach the specified math concepts.

CLASSROOM MOTIVATION AND MANAGEMENT

Standard #5

The teacher uses an understanding of individual and group motivation and behavior to create a learning environment that encourages positive social interaction, active engagement in learning, and self-motivation.

Explanation of the Standard

Effective teachers work in many ways to build positive classroom interactions. These teachers recognize that involving students in this endeavor not only promotes growth in personal and social responsibility but also enhances the development of democratic and social values. Group rapport is enhanced as students and teachers work cooperatively to establish classroom norms and rules. Teaching and modeling effective problem-solving techniques such as conflict resolution provide motivation for learning, positive social interaction among children, and positive self-esteem for all. Thus, the effective teacher strives to create a learning community that fosters group decision making, collaboration, individual responsibility, and self-directed learning.

Teachers interested in building and sustaining a positive learning climate are aware of the range of behavioral phenomena confronting them. They recognize that there are situations in which the teacher will be confronted by students who are unable to function within the parameters established by the group. In these instances, teachers must rely upon their knowledge of the principles and strategies of behavior management and issues related to all aspects of motivation. As reflective practitioners, teachers use this knowledge of theory, along with their classroom experiences, to construct an ever-evolving student motivation and management philosophy. This philosophy is specific enough to guide classroom actions yet flexible enough to accommodate the individual needs of students. Therefore, effective classroom managers understand the need to be able to define problems, identify alternatives, choose a course of action and a plan for implementation, and consider the possible consequences of a given action. The teaching scenario that follows shows how a preservice teacher was able to assess his ability to create a positive learning environment and modify his own teaching behaviors to improve the climate of his classroom.

Teaching Scenario

While enrolled in an early field experience class, Michael has the opportunity to spend a few hours every week in a daycare classroom working with children ages three to five. Michael soon realizes that these young children can be very impetuous and need a great deal of support from teachers in developing self-control and learning how to function in a group.

The college instructor in the class addresses "Promoting Positive Guidance" as one of her seminar topics. In class, Michael and his classmates practice phrasing requests and directions to young children in a positive, encouraging way that would invite the children's cooperation and teach them problem-solving and negotiating skills. Michael values this instruction a great deal because he realizes that he has a tendency to be directive and often negative with children, using a great many "don'ts." Michael decides to systematically practice these positive guidance techniques in the classroom with children.

He asks a fellow classmate who is doing field work with him at the daycare center to observe and record any negative, discouraging, or demanding comments that he makes to the children. After receiving her observations, Michael reflects on how he could have communicated those same requests to the children in a positive, encouraging way. Gradually, Michael finds he is gaining in his ability to spontaneously use positive verbal guidance. He is also becoming more likely to invite problem solving rather than solve problems through correcting children.

Michael is proud of this growth; he can see how his behavior is resulting in a much better rapport with these children and is helping to create a more positive social climate. Michael decides to document this work. He includes in his portfolio a videotape of his interactions with the group, anecdotal records of his growth based on the observations of his classmate, and the following rationale statement.

Sample Cover Sheet

Artifact for Standard #5: Classroom Motivation and Management

Name of Artifact: Evidence of Positive Verbal Guidance
Date: March 4, XXXX
Course: ECE 203 – Field Experiences with Young Children
Rationale Statement:

I have chosen to use two documents that indicate the growth I have attained in understanding how to create a positive learning environment with very young children. The first is a set of anecdotal records of interactions I had in a classroom of three- to five-year-olds and my reflections on the outcomes of those interactions. The anecdotal records show growth in my ability to formulate positive, encouraging requests and responses to children. The second is a videotape of myself near the end of the field experience showing informal conversations with children and a teacher-directed activity. In this videotape, I demonstrate my ability to gain children's cooperation by the way I speak with them. I also demonstrate how I help the children solve problems with their peers, encouraging cooperation rather than taking over the situation. The strategies I am employing lead to positive social interaction and positive individual and group motivation.

COMMUNICATION SKILLS

Standard #6

The teacher uses knowledge of effective verbal, nonverbal, and media communication techniques to foster active inquiry, collaboration, and supportive interaction in the classroom.

Explanation of the Standard

Much of teaching is about sending and receiving messages. Carefully planned and skillfully delivered messages can issue invitations to students that school is a place to share ideas, investigate, create, and collaborate with others. School can be a place to be understood as well as a place to gain understanding. But without intentional considerations and planning, the messages actually received by the students can be conflicting, confusing, or discouraging. For this reason, teachers need to monitor their personal verbal and nonverbal communication so it is characterized by clarity, organization, enthusiasm, and sensitivity. Teachers' oral and written communications need to be models of appropriate grammar, content, and syntax. Effective teachers consistently use active listening skills as well. These include the use of paraphrasing, perception checking, and clarifying questions.

Environments and resources, as well as people, send messages. The physical environment of a classroom can communicate to students many things. Bright, cheerful, colorful environments are likely to set expectations that this is a happy, interesting place to be. Classrooms where all of the students have work displayed is likely to communicate that all the children share this room and all are valued. When materials that are frequently used are stored so they are easily accessible, students learn that they can be independent in this classroom. The condition and organization of materials also communicate the importance the teacher attaches to the work that is done with those materials. Part of the effective teacher's role, therefore, is to select, adapt, and create a physical environment and a broad range of instructional resources that engage the students in exciting learning and that send the messages intended.

Effective teachers also recognize the increasing importance of technology as a tool for student learning and as a major communication resource to be developed. Technological media, classroom environment, and the teacher's verbal and nonverbal communication should all work together to send the students clear and consistent messages about classroom expectations, goals, and challenges. The following scenario describes how one student teacher came to appreciate the importance of one of these aspects of effective communication: giving clear verbal directions.

Teaching Scenario

Before her student teaching experience in a kindergarten classroom, Nicole has not really considered the importance of lesson clarity. However, Nicole's first assignment teaching a game with this class brings the need for clarity home emphatically. Nicole's first direction for the game is for the children to get into a "u-shaped circle." The children know what a circle is, and most know what a "u" is. But they do not understand the term "u-shaped circle." As the children struggle to comply, Nicole keeps repeating this one directive. It is fully ten minutes before the intended semicircle is achieved. Unfortunately, it is not achieved without the cooperating teacher stepping in and physically placing the children. Nicole realizes after that experience that students need unambiguous, specific directions and that these are not always easy to formulate.

Nicole thinks that this need for clarity is unique to very young children until she reflects on instances in college courses in which she has been frustrated by vague, indefinite assignments and activity directions. Nicole determines that for all her future lessons, she will strive for clarity in every instruction as well as in presentations of information.

Nicole's greatest challenge in lesson clarity comes when planning a cooperative learning activity, which requires small groups of children to collaborate while assembling a terrarium. Nicole knows the result depends on the children fully understanding the steps to the procedure and their roles in the activity. She plans with clarity as her goal.

Later, in watching a videotape of the children collaborating to make terraria, Nicole reflects on how far she has come since the day she taught that first game. In spite of the high level of activity, the need for cooperation, the potential for messiness, and the many steps to the procedure, the terrarium lesson is a huge success. Nicole is eager to portray in her portfolio her growth in this skill of lesson clarity. The following is a copy of her cover sheet and rationale statement.

Sample Cover Sheet

Artifact for Standard #6: Communication Skills

Date: December 6, XXXX
Course: EDE 461 – Student Teaching
Rationale Statement:

I have included a lesson plan and a video of the same lesson in my portfolio to document how I achieved lesson clarity by utilizing effective verbal communication techniques. I have highlighted aspects of my lesson

plan that indicate the techniques I used to achieve clarity and foster produc-
tive, active learning and collaboration. In this lesson, I planned for lesson
clarity in a variety of ways. In the beginning, I demonstrated and discussed
the entire process of terrarium construction. Later, when the students were in
their carefully planned, heterogeneous learning groups, I reviewed the steps
again using a picture and word chart to which they could refer. We also
discussed the various jobs that could be shared among the group members
and the value of allowing everyone to help. However, rather than assigning
jobs, I allowed the groups to negotiate the assignment of these jobs. As my
video shows, the children were successful in following directions and did an
excellent job of sharing responsibilities.

INSTRUCTIONAL PLANNING SKILLS

Standard #7

The teacher plans instruction based on knowledge of subject matter, students, the community, and curriculum goals.

Explanation of the Standard

An effective teacher plans learning experiences based on a set of diverse factors, each of which influences the outcome of student learning. First, the subject matter is considered. It is important that the teacher have a thorough knowledge of the composition of the subject being taught as well as an understanding of teaching methods that are unique to that subject. Second, the individual needs of learners are of utmost importance. Teachers need to be able to create short-range and long-term plans that are linked to student needs yet be ready to respond to unanticipated classroom events and adapt those plans to ensure student progress and motivation. Third, community needs and resources are a factor in planning lessons. Each community is unique in its citizens' consensus about what is important for its children to know. As public educators, teachers need to be sensitive to these beliefs and reflect on them when making plans. Fourth, curriculum goals are important. These goals give the teacher direction in making plans. Curriculum goals have a variety of sources: Many are provided by school districts and the local community; others are created by the teacher.

As teachers engage in both long-term and short-term planning, they must be flexible enough to consider these contexts: subject matter, local school district goals, current educational issues, legal issues, family and community considerations, public policies, and community resources. Tying all these together are the interests, needs, and aptitudes of each of the students being taught. While in the classroom, teachers need to be reflective of their current practice and be open to adjustments and revisions that become necessary in working with a diverse group of students. This self-reflection is evident in the teaching scenario that follows.

Teaching Scenario

Jose is a senior in the secondary English program at a large university. In searching for ways to document this standard for his portfolio, Jose looks at all the lesson plans he has written for field classes and methods courses. He wants to choose a plan that reflects his ability to combine the needs of students with school curriculum goals and community resources. One lesson plan, written for a freshman English class in which he was a field student teacher, stands out. Its objective is to analyze the actions of the main characters of several works in contemporary fiction. Each of the books in Jose's lesson is about environmental issues portraying human carelessness with the earth. The main character in each book learns an important lesson about the environment and changes his or her behavior by recycling, conserving water, reusing household items, or encouraging community action. For Jose's lesson, the students determine what these main characters have in common. They conclude that each of them discovered the fragility of the earth and that environmental concerns are important to all people. As a concluding activity, the students begin a school recycling program and recruit community support. Through cooperative learning, groups are assigned responsibilities, and individual group members capitalize on their own personal interests to help with this plan. Some students write letters, others speak to community leaders, and still others create media advertisements. Within days, widespread awareness of a school recycling program has begun.

Sample Cover Sheet

Artifact for Standard #7: Instructional Planning Skills

Name of Artifact: "Using Literature as a Springboard for Community Action"—A Freshman English Class Lesson Plan
Date: April 12, XXXX
Course: EDU 219 – Secondary Schools Field Experiences
Rationale Statement:

Included as documentation for this outcome is a lesson plan I created for a freshman English class. I had an opportunity to teach this lesson in a field class. It integrates the subject areas of literature, science, and social studies, reflecting my knowledge of subject matter. It also meets several objectives in the curriculum guide for the school district in which I taught my field class.

In the lesson, the students read several works in contemporary young adult fiction, all of which contain the theme of protecting earth's environment. They compared the main characters of each book and concluded that it is important to recycle, conserve, and protect our natural resources. As a culminating activity, the students brainstormed ways to recycle at their own school and began implementing such a plan. This reflects information that is not only personally meaningful to the students but also important for them as citizens of their communities. Recent local community efforts in recycling made this lesson plan even more timely. While implementing this plan, which took a period of days, I used cooperative learning to help the students view each other as members of a team working toward a single goal—the school recycling program. By guiding the students to use their own strengths toward the implementation of the plan, I was allowing my lesson planning to be flexible enough to meet their individual needs and interests.

For documentation, I have included the lesson plan, a copy of the students' recycling program, a school newspaper article outlining the project, samples of student letters and advertisements, and a copy of the curriculum guide for freshman English, with specific objectives highlighted.

ASSESSMENT OF STUDENT LEARNING

Standard #8

The teacher understands and uses formal and informal assessment strategies to ensure the continuous intellectual, social, and physical development of the learner.

Explanation of Standard

The purpose of assessment is to assist students, teachers, schools, and parents in recognizing what students have learned and to identify areas in which students need improvement. Teachers gather, synthesize, and evaluate many different types of information about their students to make effective decisions about instruction.

Traditional assessment has been based on specific information that students acquire. Observations, tests on content, and standardized tests are examples of traditional evaluative measures that provide indicators that suggest learning has taken place. These traditional measures, however, may tell little about the depth of knowledge in relation to solving real-life problems. New approaches to assessment have tried to address this need by focusing on performance samples in which students demonstrate that they can perform a task such as giving a speech, playing an instrument, or writing a story. Some of these tasks are called alternative assessments because they take place in a contrived context. They are an improvised or created "alternative" to a real-life problem-solving situation. In contrast, other performance tasks are authentic assessments because students demonstrate learning in a real-life setting. For example, a student might be asked to give a speech while running for school office. If the student wants to be elected, the speech must be convincing enough to accomplish this. This type of authentic assessment measures not only the student's ability to effectively demonstrate skills or solve problems but also his ability to assume responsibility for directing his own learning. Because of the benefits of using a variety of assessment strategies, many teachers are helping students to organize their work samples into portfolios. This approach to assessment relies on work samples and performance tasks that reflect the academic growth of the student over time. A portfolio should include a variety of both authentic and alternative assessment samples. More specifically, teachers evaluate items such as learning logs, journals, criterion-referenced tests, observations, peer evaluation and self-evaluations, homework, and group projects. Whatever type of assessment is used, each should reflect the following three qualities: The assessment should be as reliable as possible. This means that the assessment should provide dependable, consistent results. In addition, the assessment strategies used by the teacher should be valid. In other words, the teacher should make sure that the assessment strategy measures what it claims to measure. Finally, the strategies should be fair, impartial, and unbiased.

The following scenario shows how a field experience student and a cooperating teacher gather, synthesize, and evaluate different types of assessment information in order to direct instruction.

Teaching Scenario

Deidre is an education major enrolled in a field experience course. She has the opportunity to spend several hours a week in a language arts class at a middle school. The school has recently adopted the concept of portfolios and now directs its efforts to collecting alternative and authentic assessment measures to evaluate student writing.

At first, Deidre observes the teacher, students, and their interaction during writing lessons. She takes notes on student reaction to the lesson and lists various writing activities the students will be working on in the coming weeks.

Her supervising teacher encourages her to take part in the assessment of the student writing process. More specifically, she suggests that Deidre focus on the writing development of one particular student. The district's annual writing assessment project takes place over several days, follows the process writing approach, and results in a final draft. The student that Deidre selected not only has completed this writing task but also has written a persuasive speech in hopes that she will be elected secretary of the student council.

Deidre begins to notice a number of activities that could be included in this student's portfolio to assess progress in writing. Deidre collects anecdotal records of the student's progress during both of these writing projects. She is invited to observe writing conferences as well as read journal and learning-log entries.

Deidre is pleased that she has had the opportunity to observe and participate in this assessment project. She has collected several samples of different types of assessment and documented all of her observations. She begins to confer with her cooperating teacher to assess the student's writing progress in the last weeks. First draft, rewrite, and final draft are sequenced to show progressive improvement. Anecdotal records and student comments in the learning log and journal entries reflect progress the student has made. With the permission of the cooperating teacher and the student, samples of this go into Deidre's portfolio. She is careful to delete the student's name and other forms of identification.

Sample Cover Sheet

Artifact for Standard #8: Assessment of Student Learning

Name of Artifact: Authentic and Alternative Assessments of a Seventh-
  Grade Writer
Date: January 2, XXXX
Course: EDE 202 – Field Experience
Rationale Statement:
  The artifacts provided in this section show the material that my cooperat-
ing teacher and I gathered in my effort to evaluate one student's writing. I
recognized the writing task as a form of alternative assessment and chose to
include developmental samples of this student's writing in my portfolio for
Standard #8.
  I also included the draft and final copy of a persuasive speech prepared
by the student, as this is an example of authentic assessment. The student's
learning log revealed her knowledge of the writing process and her strengths
and weaknesses. Journal entries reflected the enjoyment she derives from
writing. I have read the student's writing, observed the writing process,
watched presentations, reflected on the self-evaluations and peer evaluations,
and reviewed homework. As a result, I have collected a running record of this
student's growth and development in writing. My cooperating teacher and I
have gathered all the necessary samples to make a reliable, valid, unbiased
evaluation of the student's writing. This information will be used to make
effective decisions about future instruction. I have included my evaluation of
this student's progress as well as her portfolio work samples because they
show my ability to synthesize information about a student from a variety of
sources of data.

PROFESSIONAL COMMITMENT AND RESPONSIBILITY

Standard #9

The teacher is a reflective practitioner who continually evaluates the effects of his or her choices and actions on others (students, parents, and other professionals in the learning community) and who actively seeks opportunities to grow professionally.

Explanation of the Standard

A good teacher is one who has the ability to learn as much from the students as they learn from him or her. In an effort to match instruction to the needs of students, this teacher spends much time evaluating the implications of his or her teaching decisions in the classroom. This is the mark of a reflective practitioner. Such self-reflection leads to greater knowledge about the students, about the subject being taught, and about the act of teaching.

Self-reflection also takes place in considering the teacher's relationships with parents and educational professionals. The responsibilities of educators in a democratic society include that of working with a community of concerned individuals who rally around one central goal—educating children. Children learn much from their experiences within their families and the outside world. Recognizing these facts, the teacher must cultivate strong relationships with parents as well as with educational professionals, constantly reevaluating the effects of his or her decisions on all who are involved with the education of the students.

This constant evaluation of choices extends itself outside the classroom. Indeed, a teaching professional is one who has a need for continuing education. Certification is only the first step in a long process of continual development as a professional. Growing professionally means learning new ways to make lesson plans, understand subject matter more thoroughly, and manage a classroom, among hundreds of other skills. But true professionals need more than technical teaching skills. They must also have the ability to constantly self-evaluate and act critically. New ideas together with classroom experience form a stronger theoretical base from which the teacher works, allowing for more effective decision making in the classroom. Thus, it is crucial that teachers seek opportunities for professional growth and place new ideas within the theoretical framework that already exists in their classrooms.

The role of the reflective practitioner is demonstrated in the following scenario of Mary, an elementary preservice teacher. Note how Mary utilizes the skills of reflection and critical decision making in order to meet the needs of her students and to engage in professional growth with colleagues.

Teaching Scenario

Mary, a preservice teacher, is completing her student teaching experience at Green Valley Elementary School. One student, Michael, in her third-grade class, has been diagnosed with several emotional problems, which are affecting his academic work. While teaching this class, Mary is constantly challenged to meet this child's needs. She keeps a journal in which she records her daily activities while student teaching as well as her thoughts and reactions to classroom life. In this journal, she makes several entries about Michael's responses to her teaching decisions, making sure to keep his identity anonymous. She realizes that she would like to know more about how to help Michael succeed. She makes an appointment with the school psychologist, Dr. Rose, to discuss this. Dr. Rose makes several suggestions, which Mary documents in her journal. Mary asks her cooperating teacher if she may schedule a conference with Michael's parents to share ideas and learn more about how his behavior at home may be affecting his schoolwork. His parents, impressed with her professionalism, wrote her a note praising her dedication to helping their son. In addition, Mary checks out several books on the subject of emotional disabilities in the classroom and makes note of some of the suggestions outlined there. At the university, Mary leads a discussion in her student-teaching seminar on this subject, based on what she has learned in her reading. She creates a handout of suggestions and shares this with her classmates.

Mary decides to document Standard #9 with evidence of her experiences. She inserts the journal entries, thank-you note from the parents, bibliography of books on the subject, and handout from the seminar into her portfolio. Her cover sheet and rationale statement follow.

Sample Cover Sheet

Artifact for Standard #9: Professional Commitment and Responsibility

Name of Artifact: Collection of Documents on Emotional Disabilities in School
Date: May 21, **XXXX**
Course: EDU 410 – Student Teaching
Rationale Statement:

My student-teaching experience presented me with a challenge. I worked with a little boy who was experiencing emotional difficulties that prevented him from succeeding in the classroom. I felt it was important for me to learn more about what I could do to help improve his classroom experiences, so I sought additional information. A visit with the school psychologist, a conference with the parents, and the reading of several books on the subject helped to add to my knowledge of how to teach this youngster and others like him. I shared this information in a seminar discussion with my classmates and found that many of them had the same challenges. We were able to share more ideas as the discussion progressed. I gave them a handout I prepared, outlining several teaching suggestions learned from my investigation of this problem. This handout is included as documentation of this standard.

In addition, I have included my journal entries, which outline some of the questions I had about working with this child as well as some of the things I learned during my discussions with the school psychologist. A thank-you note the parents wrote after our conference is included because it shows my commitment to building strong relationships with the family. Finally, a bibliography of books on emotional disabilities is included because it shows the research that I did to improve my knowledge of the subject.

PARTNERSHIPS

Standard #10

The teacher fosters relationships with school colleagues, parents, and agencies in the larger community to support students' learning and well-being.

Explanation of the Standard

Effective teachers engage in a variety of experiences within and beyond the school that promote a spirit of collaboration, collegiality, and personal growth. They work in cooperative teams, endorse collegial efforts, and seek opportunities to work with parents and the community at large. These teachers recognize the importance of sharing experiences and ideas.

As teachers expand their realm of interactions, they recognize how cultural identity plays an important part in the way others react to the world, how they learn, and how they view themselves. Community members and events can be powerful teachers of teachers. Effective teachers learn how to successfully use churches, civic, and community-based organizations as resources and as ways of motivating and encouraging positive growth in students. Exposure to these influences can assist teachers in understanding the frame of reference within which the community's children operate. Connecting the school and community requires that the teacher integrate multicultural education throughout the curriculum. Teachers must be receptive to moving beyond the walls of the school and opening the door to discover the students' other learning environments. The following scenario illustrates how Linda, a secondary mathematics education major, enhanced her student-teaching experiences and promoted the well-being of her students through collaboration and partnerships with colleagues, parents, and the larger community.

Teaching Scenario

Linda, a math major in secondary education, has completed her student teaching in the Springfield City School District. She enjoyed the diversity she experienced among her assignments in the tenth- to twelfth-grade classrooms at Greenview High School. In addition to her teaching assignments, Linda became involved in an important school–community project.

During her first month at the school, she joined the after-school tutoring team, sponsored by the Parent–Teacher Organization (PTO). This program prepares parents and older adults to tutor students. When she was not busy training tutors, Linda would often work with small groups of students. On

several occasions, Linda was assigned responsibility for contacting new parent volunteers and orienting them to the guidelines and curriculum of the
program. Her work with the PTO led Linda to several community agencies.
One of the PTO members introduced her to the coordinator of the Springfield Parent Partnership Organization, an alternative education program for
single parents. Linda was able to interview several parents, recruiting them
for the tutoring program. She also visited and interviewed the staff at the
Children's Hospital Family Crisis Center and at the Springfield Drug and
Alcohol Rehabilitation Center. These experiences helped Linda better understand the needs of some of her students as well as the dynamics of the
community in which they live.

Linda gathers artifacts documenting these experiences for Standard #10
in her portfolio. She wishes to demonstrate how she endeavored to foster
relationships with school colleagues, parents, and agencies in the larger
community, and to support students' learning and well-being.

Sample Cover Sheet

Artifact for Standard #10: Partnerships

Name of Artifact: Collection of Documents from Work with PTO After-
    School Tutoring Program
Date: December 12, XXXX
Course: EDE 461 – Student Teaching
Rationale Statement:

While student teaching at Greenview High School, I became involved in
the After-School Tutoring program, sponsored by the PTO. To document
my work, I have included my "Volunteer's Log and Journal," which chronicles
the experiences I had with the students as well as with the parent volunteers.
Also included are samples of student work and a packet of materials I created
to use in training parent volunteers for tutoring services.

My visits to the Springfield Parent Partnership program, the Children's
Hospital Family Crisis Center, and the Springfield Drug and Alcohol Rehabilitation Center are documented with letters of inquiry and thank-you notes.
The purpose of these visits was to enhance our tutoring program by reaching
out to potential volunteers as well as to students in need.

Lastly, I have included a certificate of appreciation from the Greenview
PTO. All of these documents portray my ability to coordinate the efforts of
parents and community members in the interest of helping students who need
tutorial aid in high school. I believe that programs of this type are most
successful when there is a thorough understanding of the impact the commu-

nity has on its children and when there is a partnership between the school and its neighboring agencies. My work with the PTO and its After-School Tutoring program reflects my commitment to this belief.

4

ARTIFACTS
POSSIBILITIES

HOW TO USE THIS CHAPTER

The types of documents listed on the next few pages are possible artifacts for your portfolio. They are explained here so that you may better facilitate their use. Each definition contains two features: a definition of the document as it relates to classes and other learning opportunities, and an explanation of the types of teaching skills that this document may reflect. These suggestions do not include all the possibilities that exist as documents. As you create artifacts that make reference to students or teachers, avoid using names or other identifying information. It is always critical to maintain confidentiality.

TYPES OF ARTIFACTS

Anecdotal Records

These are notes that you have taken in classroom observations or during your own teaching. They may pertain to any of the following: the intellectual, social, emotional, or physical development of a child or some children; personal observations about instructional decisions that you have made; or personal observations of teachers at work. The notes reflect your assessment or child observation skills, your ability to make instructional plans, or your knowledge of child development.

Article Summaries or Critiques

As a class assignment, you may have written a summary or evaluation of an article from a professional journal. When including these in your portfolio, choose critiques that address the desired topic very specifically. The title of the article should be reflective of a chosen standard, making an obvious connection. This document is especially helpful if your professor has made positive remarks about your work, and these remarks are about the outcome you wish to document.

The article summary or critique may show your ability to analyze any number of teaching skills. For example, suppose you critiqued an article titled "Getting Parents Involved in Their Children's Education." If you discussed your own ideas about parent involvement in your critique, this document may be able to reflect your knowledge of school–home–community cooperation.

Assessments

Any forms of assessment you have used or developed to measure child performance would be included in this type of document. Examples of assessments are: performance tasks, portfolios, teacher-written tests, informal observations or notes, evaluations from lesson plans, formative assessment notes or charts, and summative charts of student developmental levels. You may want to include the actual assessment instrument you have written, with the children's work on it, if applicable (only one copy is necessary). In addition, you may include notes in a personal journal from observations made during the administration of a standardized test.

Your ability to assess children's performance, diagnose progress, and use tests wisely is reflected in this document. In addition, your understanding of child development may be evident.

Awards and Certificates

Copies of letters, awards, or certificates that verify your outstanding contribution to the field of education fit in this category. These could include: honors conferred, memberships in honorary professional organizations, community recognition, and volunteer recognition. Your professional commitment is reflected in these types of documents.

Bulletin Board Ideas

After creating a bulletin board, make a copy of your design or take a photograph of a bulletin board you have created. Make sure all spelling, punctuation, and grammar are Standard English. This document may be used to show your ability to think creatively, use materials in interesting ways, or motivate students.

Case Studies

A case study is a thorough examination of a student's growth over a period of time. When using this as a document, make sure the student is anonymous. Generally, case studies are quite long; therefore, you may want to include a specific part of the paper for documentation of a standard. Your knowledge of child development as well as your observation skills may be evident in this document.

Classroom Management Philosophy

This is a written summary of your philosophy regarding classroom management. Make sure to cite the research and theories that have guided you in the way you influence student behavior and encourage development of self-control. Classroom management skills and knowledge of human development are evident in this document.

Community Resources Documents

These might include copies of actual correspondence or a description of less formal contact between you and a community resource. Have you solicited a community resource to provide information in completing a course assignment or to teach a lesson in the classroom? Did you invite a guest speaker into your classroom during a field class or student teaching? These types of correspondence show that you are able to foster positive relationships between the community and the school.

Computer Programs

This includes examples of various programs you have utilized, developed, or incorporated in your teaching, which provide evidence of your ability to use materials in a challenging and appropriate manner to encourage active learning.

Also appropriate are programs that demonstrate your ability to conduct on-line searches and research. Examples include ERIC, Education Index, and Internet programs that link teachers worldwide. You can document your abilities by providing the hard copies of these searches along with an explanation of the reason for your computer searches. These documents reflect your willingness to seek further professional growth.

Cooperative Learning Strategies

Have you planned or taught a lesson using a cooperative learning technique? Cooperative learning is a method of teaching in which students work collaboratively in small groups to solve a problem. This type of group work must be obvious in your lesson. You may want to include a copy of the lesson plan and, if the lesson was actually taught, a statement assessing the effectiveness of the cooperative learning technique. This will document your ability to use cooperative learning as a strategy as well as your ability to manage and motivate a class of students.

Curriculum Plans

These documents are written plans, or programs, or both designed to organize curriculum. Your curriculum plans can reflect all experiences you have developed for the child while engaged in the process of schooling. Examples may include: lesson plans, units, thematic units, learning centers, extracurricular programs, or school–community ventures. These documents portray your instructional planning skills or your ability to use many and varied instructional strategies.

Essays

You can use papers from education courses, English composition, or any other class in which you were required to write an essay. Examine the topic you addressed in your paper to be sure its main idea reflects one of the standards you are using.

This type of artifact could document almost any standard. A question you wish to answer or the topic you wish to address should be clearly stated at the beginning of the essay. You may want to highlight this, showing its obvious connection to the standard you wish to document. For example, suppose you wrote an essay in a composition class titled "Why Suzy Can't Do Math: The Influence of Societal Expectations." Because this is an essay on the differences that gender may make in the perception of students in the home, in the neighborhood, and in school, your understanding of social influences on the education of females becomes evident. This would be a good artifact to document your understanding of the multiple contexts affecting educational decisions.

Evaluations

Any on-the-job performance assessment is an especially important type of evaluation to include in a portfolio. Student teaching is one place where this will occur. You might include actual observations done when you taught a lesson, feedback on a written assignment, or some kind of summative assessment (interim or final evaluation). Make sure there is a relationship between the evaluation comments and the standard.

Field Trip Plans

As a preservice teacher, you may have gone on field trips that would be related to one of the standards you have chosen to use. Trips such as these may include visits to teacher centers, libraries, museums, innovative classrooms, other universities, youth centers, rehabilitation centers, or church-related activities. You may document this by including copies of programs, personal journals, agenda, letters of invitation, or memos. Your own notes or observational reports are also helpful. This type of document may provide evidence for a variety of standards. Your professional commitment and responsibility are reflected because of your willingness to seek information outside the college classroom.

You may have attended field trips with a student group. This experience may document one of the standards, depending on the nature of the trip and your reaction to it. A well-written reaction paper or journal entry would help document such a trip. For example, suppose you were invited to join your field class on a trip to the children's theater. Your cooperating teacher did a nice job of incorporating this trip into her classroom lessons by reading a book about the play to the children, then having them act it out themselves and write an experience story about the trip. If you write an observational report about this, making notes about the interrelatedness of the activities and the importance of the subject matter to the growth of the students, you can document your knowledge of content and of child development.

If you actually planned a field trip for one of your classes, be sure to document this. Record your lesson plans, your correspondence with the community agents involved, your letter to parents, and any other communication you used. This is strong evidence of your planning skills, knowledge of content, knowledge of human development, and school–home–community cooperation.

Floor Plans

This includes a sketch of the arrangement of space, equipment, and materials you designed in order to meet the needs of a group of students under your supervision. Your ability to use environments and materials appropriately is most closely related to this document. If you also include a statement of how this floor plan enhances your classroom management plan, then it also could document your classroom management skills.

Goal Statements

Professional goals are based on your needs, your interest, your philosophy of education, and your perception of your role as a teacher. Goal statements assist you in determining where you want to be and provide you with information about how to get there.

Think about the important results you should accomplish in your role as a teacher and record these as goal statements. Remember that any short-term goals you establish should be tied to the longer-term goals you have identified in conjunction with your philosophy of education. Periodically review and evaluate your accomplishments in relation to your goal statements. You may wish to list your accomplishments associated with each goal. You will establish new goals as you refine your philosophy of education, your role as a teacher, and your expectations. It is important to keep your list of goal statements current. These statements might appear at the beginning of your portfolio or as documentation of your professional commitment.

Individualized Plans

Children with special needs at times need tasks to be structured in ways that will allow them to use their strengths and compensate for their specific learning difficulties. Ways in which lesson and unit plans have been adapted for specific students should be documented. Make sure the learning need is defined and clearly addressed. This artifact could document your skills in meeting individual needs, your instructional strategies skills, your knowledge of child development.

Interviews with Students, Teachers, Parents

These include planned conversations with a specific agenda. Include a copy of the questions and answers as well as a summary and analysis of the interview. This interview may be part of a case study for one of your classes. Interviews can yield a variety of information; for example, an interview with a student may give you some indication of his or her language development, thus documenting your understanding of human development.

Journals

You may have kept journals during field classes or observation assignments. Include them if they address your observations of students as they relate to the desired standard. If necessary, highlight the appropriate sections of the journals. Make sure dates and times are included but not the names of schools or teachers visited.

Lesson Plans

Copies of your lesson plans should include all components of a workable plan: objectives, materials, introduction, procedures, closing, and evaluation.

Sometimes plans may be used for more than one standard. In this case, highlight the specific part of the plan that documents the outcome. Your ability to execute instructional planning and to use a variety of instructional strategies will be most obviously documented with lesson plans; however, it is possible that knowledge of content, use of environments and materials, communication skills, and knowledge of human development could be documented here.

Letters to Parents

Include copies of correspondence that were sent home. This could include: permission slips, weekly newsletters, requests for parental help with homework, notices about parties, notification about field trips, requests for parent conferences, student award certificates, or letters that explain upcoming activities. Such correspondence could document your cooperation with the home and community. Make sure letters contain correct spelling and Standard English grammar.

Management and Organization Strategies

After trying a particular management or classroom organization strategy, systematically observe and code the events that occurred. This will enable you to record what is important about your experience. Write a brief summary and explanation of your observation. For example, you may have tried a chart system for classroom jobs, a record-keeping device for holistic scoring of writing, a system of recording anecdotal notes, or a way to expedite peer editing during writing classes. These types of explanations reflect your ability to manage the classroom well.

Media Competencies

This type of document includes evidence and descriptions of the various forms of media you are able to incorporate in your instruction. This could include teaching resources such as the slide projector, camcorder and VCR, overhead projector, 16mm projector, computers and printers, interactive video, laser disks, and cable and electronic (educational) television.

You will also want to include evidence of your ability to incorporate technology into the classroom. Examples of how you have used e-mail, remote data bases, and distance learning equipment to research and to communicate with students and colleagues regionally, nationally, and internationally should be highlighted. A printout or floppy disk of your Internet address(es), listing of professional on-line news group and listserve memberships you hold, and examples of printed texts will provide documentation of your ability to share and retrieve information via Internet.

Media competency reflects your ability to utilize a wide range of communication resources, environments, and materials appropriately. Therefore, you may wish to include a checklist of the various media and other state-of-the-art technology you are able to incorporate into your classroom.

Meetings and Workshops Log

If you have attended meetings or listened to speakers who discussed a topic related to the standard, include a reaction paper plus a copy of the program. These logs would be a good way to document your professional commitment and responsibility.

Observation Reports

Systematic, regular noticing and recording of behaviors, events, and interactions in the classroom should be a part of every field experience you have. Include brief descriptions of your observations in a variety of grade levels. Reports could be in paragraph or checklist format. Depending upon the focus of your observations, your reports may reflect your knowledge of a variety of standards.

Peer Critiques

This encompasses formal and informal assessments of you by your classmates. This could include score reports that are made out by classmates during your class presentations. The standard you document with this artifact depends on the presentation that your peers critique. If it was a lesson demonstration, your planning or instructional strategies skills would be evident. Your use of materials, communication skills, or knowledge of human development might also be evident. Make sure the comments made by your peers reflect the standard you are documenting.

Philosophy Statement

This is a brief position paper or statement of your philosophy of teaching. Make it clear and concrete. Preface your entire portfolio with this statement. Sometimes it is an assignment in a class but if not, write one on your own. It should include your underlying beliefs about the teaching strategies and practices that are best for students. Either leave out or explain educational jargon; do not include such terms simply because they sound good. If you include this in more than one section, highlight the part that pertains to the specific standard.

Pictures and Photographs

Include photographs that show active learning in progress, special projects, field trips, or artistic expressions that cannot be physically included in this notebook because of size. Bulletin boards, puppets, learning centers, and trips to museums are just some of the many ideas and activities you may want to photograph.

Depending on the photograph, you could document a variety of standards. If it is of a field trip that you took to a professional meeting or conference, document your professional commitment. If it is of a field trip or other related activity in which you participated with a class of students, you may want to document your use of instructional strategies, depending on your involvement in the planning process.

Portfolio (Student)

A student portfolio is an organized collection of a student's work that demonstrates the student's achievement and performance over time. Various kinds of evidence might be used, including the student's projects, written work, learning journals, and video demonstrations. A sample student portfolio would document your ability to use a variety of assessment strategies.

Position Papers

Include scholarly papers written to defend an educational issue, viewpoint, or controversy. Be sure that sources are up-to-date. (No source should go back beyond five years.) Papers such as these could document your professional commitment as well as your knowledge of philosophical and social influences.

Problem-Solving Logs

As you identify professional problems or challenges, record them. It would be helpful to include: a clear statement of the problem, alternative strategies for dealing with the problem, the chosen strategies, and the results of the implementation of each of them. Depending on the problem you solved, document your use of instructional strategies, classroom management skills, or your cooperation with the home and community.

Professional Development Plans

Include a short paragraph or list explaining your short- and long-term plans for professional development. This could include efforts to improve knowledge or performance in specific areas of teaching, attendance and participation in professional organizations or workshops, and plans for earning additional credits in graduate school. This area should be reflective of where you are now in terms of your profession and where you plan to be within the next few years. Such statements document your professional commitment and responsibility.

Professional Organizations and Committees List

List and briefly describe your involvement with an organization, committee, or other group that you feel has had an impact on you professionally or personally. Examples could include participation in campus and community organizations. Be sure to include some sort of evidence of your participation in these groups, such as a membership card, a letter of acceptance, or program from an activity. Such memberships show that you actively seek out opportunities to grow professionally.

Professional Readings List

Keep a list of professional readings you have done and include your reactions to the issues and concepts discussed. Your professional commitment and responsibility are reflected in professional reading lists.

Projects

Projects can include any type of assignment that involved problem solving, group presentations, creating materials, investigating phenomena in classrooms, or researching current information. In a presentation portfolio, include paper copies only and make photographs of anything too large to fit in a notebook. If this is a group project, make that clear but indicate the extent of your input. (Be careful about this one; it is not helpful to brag about doing all the work.)

The documentation possibilities of this artifact depend on the project. Examine the standards to determine whether the project reflects instructional planning skills, professional commitment, the ability to meet individual needs, or knowledge of content.

References

References might include statements, or evaluations, or both, from your supervisors of your academic work, experiences in the classroom, other work experience with children, or outside employment.

Try to connect the reference with one of your selected standards. For instance, the reference might describe a lesson you taught in a field course or in student teaching. You could use this document to illustrate your competence in the area of instructional strategies. In addition, you may want to place reference letters from your cooperating teachers in a special tabbed section of the notebook.

Research Papers

When selecting a research paper to include in your portfolio, you will need to consider several factors. The content of the research paper might make it appropriate for inclusion under a particular standard. It might, for instance, highlight your knowledge of an academic subject.

Rules and Procedures Descriptions

While you were student teaching or perhaps during field classes, you may have had the opportunity to write your own classroom rules or procedures. These should describe the regular, repeated guidelines or routines for behavior that give your classroom predictability and order. These descriptions of rules should give some evidence of your ability to manage the classroom and create an environment conducive to learning and positive interaction.

Schedules

During student teaching, you were probably asked to complete a daily schedule. If you use this as a document, be sure that it clearly describes your format for the events of the day for students under your supervision. The order of events and the length of time allotted to each should be clear and concise. Classroom management skills are reflected in this type of artifact.

Seating Arrangement Diagrams

A particular seating arrangement (such as having students sit in groups) might complement a particular teaching strategy (such as cooperative learning). It might also reflect a particular classroom management need, such as seating certain students apart from the rest of the class. Thus, your ability to plan for instruction, use environments, and manage the classroom could be documented with this artifact.

Self-Assessment Instruments

This includes results from instruments, rating scales, surveys, or questionnaires that provide feedback regarding your performance. This shows your professional commitment and responsibility. Self-assessment instruments also include examples of instruments you developed to engage students in measuring their own performance (cognitive, affective, and psychomotor). These could document your assessment skills.

Simulated Experiences

Include an explanation of educational experiences in which you learned through the use of simulation as a teaching method. A simulation is an activity that represents a real-life experience. This activity could include teaching an elementary lesson in a methods class, dramatizing a simulated classroom management scenario, or some other type of role-play experience.

Describe the simulation, its purpose, and what you feel you learned from the experience. The simulation itself will determine the standard you can document here.

Student Contracts

You may have the opportunity to write individual (one-on-one) contracts to help promote a student's academic achievement or improved behavior. The actual "contract" should look formal—it should be typed and specifically spell out the conditions under which the terms of the contract (achievement, behavior, and so on) will be met. In addition, it should include a space for the teacher as well as the student to sign, date, and confirm their agreement to the conditions. You may not have the need to draw up contracts until you student teach, but you may see some in use during your field experiences. (Classroom management rules that all students are expected to follow do not qualify under this category.) This type of artifact reflects your ability to develop learning experiences on the basis of diagnosis and observation, or perhaps it can document your classroom management skills, depending on the reason for the individual contract.

Subscriptions

If you subscribe to a journal that specifically addresses the standard in its title, include a copy of the cover of the journal, along with the address label showing your name. You might also briefly mention any ideas, instructional techniques, or other helpful information you gathered from reading the journal. Generally, professional commitment is well documented with subscriptions; however, you may find other standards to document with this artifact, depending on the type of journal to which you subscribe.

Teacher-Made Materials

These materials may include games, manipulatives, puppets, big books, charts, videotapes, films, photographs, transparencies, teaching aids, costumes, posters, or artwork. Since many of these items are cumbersome, include only paper copies or photographs of the materials. If you do not have copies of the actual materials you have made, you may want to highlight sections of a well-designed lesson plan that show how you would use creative teaching materials. Materials that support learning theory and were designed to suit this purpose are most helpful. Your materials should reflect your ability to encourage active learning and a variety of instructional strategies.

Theme Studies

This is a set of lesson plans or resource materials that fit a central theme. Theme studies integrate many subjects, which might include math, science, health, physical education, English, social studies, reading, art, music, and spelling. Make sure that your plans contain all elements of good lesson plans and are obviously related to your overall theme. Your knowledge of a variety of instructional strategies should be evident through your use of computer programs, children's literature, manipulatives, films, charts, or concrete materials. In addition, your instructional planning skills will be evident.

Transcripts

A copy of your official transcript can be used in a variety of ways. You may wish to use it to document your knowledge in subject areas such as chemistry, geography, or education courses. Highlight the courses and the grade you wish to document. Include a brief, typewritten explanation of why this transcript is included. You may even include other information, such as a syllabus from the course that you have highlighted, to show that you have taken essay or other types of tests on the subject.

Unit Plans

A unit plan is an integrated plan for instruction on a topic developed over several days or even weeks. Often, units are developed within a discipline, and lessons are organized to build on knowledge acquired in previous lessons. Unit plans generally include purposes, objectives, content outlines, activities, instructional resources, and evaluation methods. (Interdisciplinary units have been described under an entry called Theme Studies.) Unit plans are particularly good for documenting your ability to use a variety of instructional strategies and instructional planning skills.

Video Scenario Critiques

Often in college methods courses, professors will ask you to view and critique a videotape of actual teaching scenarios. If you wish to include a critique you have completed, be sure to describe the scenario and give its bibliographical information. Make sure the critique speaks to the standard you plan to document. Depending on the nature of the video, there are several possibilities for documentation.

Volunteer Experience Descriptions

This document might include a list and brief description of volunteer experiences and services provided to the school and community. You should focus on how these activities have enhanced your abilities while providing a contribution to society. You should also emphasize the importance of maintaining positive school–community collaboration through teacher, parent, and student interaction. Depending on what you learned from these experiences, make sure they address the standard under which you have placed this document.

Work Experience Descriptions

These are statements you have written to describe work experiences. These might include work with students in both traditional and nontraditional settings and work for which you were compensated or that you performed on a voluntary basis. To be of most interest, these statements should include not only a summary of the setting and your responsibilities but also a reflective statement addressing the intangible aspects of the work experience. In writing these statements, be sure to address how these work experiences relate to the specific standard.

Appendix A

PROFESSIONAL ORGANIZATIONS

Many professional organizations are working on developing standards for teachers. Because these organizations are in various stages of this process, we recommend that you write directly to the organization(s) most appropriate to your area of teaching and request their most current set of teacher standards. In addition to the list of organizations provided below, individual state departments of education and individual colleges of teacher education are likely sources of standards. One of the best sources to contact is the National Board of Professional Teaching Standards, which is working on more than thirty categories of teacher standards.

American Alliance for Health, Physical Education, Recreation and Dance, 1900 Association Drive, Reston VA 22091.

American Association of School Librarians, 50 E. Huron Street, Chicago, IL 60611.

Association for Childhood Education International, 3615 Wisconsin Avenue NW, Washington, DC 20016.

Association for Computers in Mathematics and Science Teaching, P.O. Box 4455, Austin, TX 78765.

Association for Supervision and Curriculum Development, 125 N. West Street, Alexandria, VA 22314.

Council for Early Childhood Professional Recognition, 1718 Connecticut Avenue, NW, Washington, DC 20009.

Council for Exceptional Children, 1920 Association Drive, Reston, VA 22091.

Council for Library Resources, One Dupont Circle, Washington, DC 20036.

Council on Teaching Foreign Languages, Six Executive Plaza, Yonkers, NY 10701.

International Reading Association, 800 Barksdale Road, Newark, DE 19711.

Music Educators National Conference, 1902 Association Drive, Reston, VA 22091.

National Art Education Association, 1916 Association Drive, Reston, VA 22091.

National Association of Biology Teachers, 11250 Roger Bacon Drive, Reston, VA 22091.

National Association for the Education of Young Children, 1834 Connecticut Avenue NW, Washington, DC 20009.

National Association of Geology Teachers, P.O. Box 368, Lawrence, KS 66044.

National Board for Professional Teaching Standards, 1900 M. Street North, Suite 210, Washington, DC 20036.

National Council for the Social Studies, 3501 Newark Street NW, Washington, DC 20016.

National Council of Teachers of English, 1111 Kenyon Road, Urbana, IL 61801.

National Council of Teachers of Mathematics, 1906 Association Drive, Reston, VA 22091.

National Science Teachers Association, 1742 Connecticut Avenue NW, Washington, DC 20009.

Phi Delta Kappa, Eighth Street and Union Avenue, Bloomington, IN 47401.

Appendix B

ARTIFACTS CHECKLIST

	1	2	3	4	5	6	7	8	9	10
Anecdotal Records										
Article Summaries or Critiques										
Assessments										
Awards and Certificates										
Bulletin Board Ideas										
Case Studies										
Classroom Management Philosophy										
Community Resources Documents										
Computer Programs										

continued

	1	2	3	4	5	6	7	8	9	10
Cooperative Learning Strategies										
Curriculum Plans										
Essays										
Evaluations										
Field Trip Plans										
Floor Plans										
Goal Statements										
Individualized Plans										
Interviews with Students, Teachers, Parents										
Journals										
Lesson Plans										
Lettters to Parents										
Management and Organization Strategies										
Media Competencies										
Meetings and Workshops Log										
Observation Reports										
Peer Critiques										

	1	2	3	4	5	6	7	8	9	10
Philosophy Statement										
Pictures and Photographs										
Portfolio (Student)										
Position Papers										
Problem-Solving Logs										
Professional Development Plans										
Professional Organizations and Committees List										
Professional Readings List										
Projects										
References										
Research Papers										
Rules and Procedures Descriptions										
Schedules										
Seating Arrangement Diagrams										
Self-Assessment Instruments										
Simulated Experiences										

continued

	1	2	3	4	5	6	7	8	9	10
Student Contracts										
Subscriptions										
Teacher-Made Materials										
Theme Studies										
Transcripts										
Unit Plans										
Video Scenario Critiques										
Volunteer Experience Descriptions										
Work Experience Descriptions										